CW01095992

Century Maths

User's Guide

Gareth Buckland   **Anna Morris**

Stanley Thornes (Publishers) Ltd

First published in 1991 by Stanley Thornes (Publishers) Ltd, Old Station Drive, Leckhampton, Cheltenham GL53 0DN, England.

British Library Cataloguing-in-Publication Data

Buckland, Gareth
 Century maths: User's guide.
 I. Title   II. Morris, Anna
 372.7

ISBN 0 7487 1159 7

Printed and bound by Ebenezer Baylis and Son Ltd

Contents

Into Century Maths

Background

For many years, the belief that 'practise makes perfect' appears to have been an adage for the teaching of mathematics. Within the past ten years, in the wake of *Mathematics Counts, Better Mathematics* and more recently, the National Curriculum, this idea has become increasingly outdated. The concept of investigational mathematics has become an active rather than a dormant ideal. Natural reservations of teachers, together with the plethora of other restraints, have limited the development of this style. Investigations currently exist in mathematics departments, but rather than considering investigations, we should address the idea of an **investigative approach** through which pupils can develop an understanding of a particular mathematical concept. This could encompass a number of different facets, including perhaps:

- exposition by the teacher
- open-ended investigations
- problem-solving
- consolidation of discovered knowledge
- the use of computers as an integral part of learning mathematics
- puzzles and games

Although an investigative approach may be seen as a journey into the unknown, pupils can often be excited by the prospect of making their own choices about the direction of their work. This, in turn, will develop the pupils' confidence in handling mathematical concepts as well as their ability to resolve more generalised problems. All too often pupils are presented with an investigation or a problem to solve as a sweetener, with mathematics being the medicine. However, through a cocktail of the approaches listed above, progress to a better understanding of mathematical concepts can be achieved.

Thinking about a New Approach?

For an effective use of material devised to stimulate pupils to think for themselves, you are probably considering not only the change in approach made by the pupils, but also the change, invoked by the materials, on yourself.

There is a need to **create** a learning environment within which pupils can work with confidence. Pupils have to feel secure in the knowledge that ideas of their own will be well-received and considered by the group. Your approach becomes one of involvement in the process of discovery with the pupils: supporting rather than directing discussion and arguments.

In this interaction, a key issue arises, that of when to **intervene** and when to step back. You are guiding pupils in formulating their own thoughts rather than giving them the content of these thoughts.

Your role becomes that of **facilitator** for the pupils' learning. Pupils at all ability levels need sufficient time, resources and opportunity for discussion, so that they become genuinely involved in the work without feeling frustration at every stumbling block. It is you, the teacher, who ensures this provision for your pupils.

Within such an atmosphere, pupils will learn:

- to think for themselves
- to work within a group situation
- to be prepared to discuss openly any viewpoint they hold
- to listen to other viewpoints and extrapolate
- to acquire confidence in sorting the relevant from the irrelevant in a mass of information, rather than seeing it as a minefield
- to be able to approach a problem from a variety of avenues
- to value the process by which they have determined their findings
- to accept that not all problems have a single 'right' answer

Using *Century Maths* to Achieve these Aims

To date, no mathematics programme or scheme has been published with the ethos expressed above. Adaptations and amendments to existing publications have taken place over the past few years, attempting to take into consideration both the demands of the GCSE and the National Curriculum for Mathematics.

Century Maths has been written from the outset with clear aims that encompass not only the philosophy explained, but also with GCSE and the National Curriculum clearly in focus.

In *Century Maths*, it is the problem that provides the motivation for the pupils — mathematical techniques are required as a means of reaching a solution. Discussing the problem, making decisions about strategies to be used and then acting as a group to resolve a situation, all form part of the learning environment fostered by the *Century Maths* programme.

This approach is supported by the structure of *Century Maths*. A series of **THEME** books has been written, each within a context which will appeal to pupils – for example *Holidays*. Each Theme book is designed to encompass all the aspects of learning mathematics listed above. Teachers and pupils are free to select the most appropriate topics within a Theme, while pupils will be able to set and work on problems of their own, leading naturally to **cross-curricular work** in a variety of subject areas.

To complement the Themes, textbooks and worksheets have been written, focused on the four main content areas of

Number (with Measures) **Algebra   Shape and Space   Handling Data**

These **FOCUS** books are designed for individual, group or class use. Although they introduce specific techniques and ideas, as well as providing opportunities to practise them, the books continue the investigative approach of the Themes and are designed to be used in parallel with them. Through the **link pages** (generally p.24 and p.48 of a Theme book), pupils can discover the mathematics resources they require to tackle problems encountered within the Theme books. As pupils develop the ideas within the Theme material, they will 'feed' their thoughts with the mathematics from within the Focus books. The more they explore the Theme, the greater the link between Theme and Focus and the larger the Theme may grow.

An important aspect of the resource to be considered is the role of **computing** within *Century Maths*. Computing based on **Logo** is integral to the whole programme. Logo forms an important part of the materials, encouraging pupils to express their mathematics in interesting and, sometimes, new ways. The computing aspect is not simply tacked on to topics, nor is it suggested when another approach is more appropriate. *Century Maths* includes a range of materials which will help pupils and teachers to exploit computing opportunities as easily as possible. Throughout the course of their work, pupils will use and extend their capabilities with Logo, either individually or in small groups. All the *Century Maths* Logo materials are fully referenced within the books.

How does *Century Maths* Help the Teacher?

The philosophy described above can only be successfully achieved with your involvement. Each pupil's book or other element in *Century Maths* has its own **Teacher's Notes**.

Each set of Teacher's Notes is fully referenced to the National Curriculum and provides detailed help with assessment and record-keeping. The accent is on assessment being unobtrusive and evolving naturally from normal classroom situations. Pupils will be involved in the assessment procedure, thus providing all concerned with:

- formative assessment of genuine value
- a record of progress
- highlighting of areas of difficulty and misconception.

A record of work covered by each individual pupil will be maintained by the pupil. This will be seen to be a constructive aspect of the learning and not merely a 'ticking boxes' activity of little meaning.

Further to these 'built-in' avenues of support, additional support for teachers using the *Century Maths* materials will be available through:

- the establishing of USER GROUPS within the locale of the schools involved
- a regular newsletter, with input from schools and *Century Maths*
- a HELPLINE, with telephone contact and contact address, particularly useful for INSET.

Through all of these support mechanisms, we aim to help you in using *Century Maths*, thus allowing you and your pupils to achieve the maximum benefit from the materials.

Century Maths *and the Primary School*

From the outset of the development of *Century Maths*, consideration was given to the diverse mathematical experiences encountered by pupils arriving at secondary school in Year 7. Through discussion groups and observation of pupils working, the *Century Maths* team worked alongside primary school teachers in attempting to appreciate the complexity of the problem of creating an entirely new mathematics resource for Years 7 – 11.

The model eventually created — interlocking Theme and Focus materials — allows pupils from a wide range of backgrounds to feel at ease with the *Century Maths* books. Year 7 pupils who previously worked within an open mathematics learning environment may feel comfortable within a Theme context, supported by the Focus books. At the same time, pupils who are accustomed to a more structured situation may feel happier concentrating on the explicitly mathematical approach of the Focus books, with shorter time allocated to Theme material. However, the underlying experience that pervades both Theme and Focus material is that of working with investigational material.

The nature of the Themes in *Century Maths* is such that they can be used across a much wider age range than those to which they have nominally been allocated. In fact, through trialling Themes in both the primary and secondary sectors, we have observed that younger and older pupils simply respond to the same Themes in different ways. The Focus books are more directed to National Curriculum attainment levels, yet the Lead-in Focus books have been trialled with similar success in primary classrooms.

Through discussion with teachers in both sectors, it is apparent that *Century Maths* is considered a suitable resource for creating a mathematics continuum for pupils crossing the primary/secondary interface. Often, primary teachers are keen to familiarise themselves and their pupils with some of the work expected at the secondary stage. It is possible that some of the Y7/8 Themes could be introduced within a primary classroom during Year 6. The necessary mathematics could be obtained either through existing primary textbooks, or through Focus books. The introduction of some Theme material at this stage, perhaps endorsed by classroom support from a teacher from the secondary school mathematics department, could enhance liaison and, at the same time, go some way towards making the educational continuum a reality.

The Framework

Using Theme and Focus books

The *Century Maths* Themes could be described as being more open-ended than the Focus books, but both are investigational in approach.

The **Themes** offer pupils the opportunity to explore problems arising from familiar situations — in some cases setting up their own problems for investigation. The Theme books for Y7/8 are:

- *Food/Animals*
- *Trees/Neighbourhood*
- *Festivals/School Fair*
- *Patterns/Ourselves*
- *Holidays/Traffic*
- *Connections/Music*

The pupils' Theme books indicate when it might be useful to set up group discussions, how to decide on the mathematics and resources to be used (e.g. appropriate use of computers), how to form plans of working, noting results, analysing them and presenting findings. To help the pupils, a series of **standard symbols (icons)** is used throughout all the Theme books. These allow the pupils to explore the mathematical content of any situation in a Theme book independently or with others. These icons are:

Special things you *will* need

Special things you *may* need

More ideas

Link page

Worksheet

Work for a computer here. (The screen may show one of these:
S – Spreadsheet **D** – Database **G** – Graph plotter **L** – Logo)

L D *Logo 2000* disk

L N *Logo 2000* documentation

L P *LogoPack*

The icon for 'Link page' (![puzzle piece icon]) will refer the pupils, through a matrix of further symbols found generally on pages 24 and 48 of each Theme book, to mathematical topic areas within the Focus books. (Link pages are described in detail on pages 12-13.)

In the Themes, some pupils may develop their own interests in consultation with their teacher, carrying the investigations beyond the suggested scope in the book. There have been many examples of this in trialling. On the other hand, some pupils may be more cautious — if they prefer to keep closer to the plan of the Theme, the book will guide them through the discussions, planning of work and final presentation of results.

Whichever way the Themes are used, **discussion of their ideas** with the teacher is seen as a key factor in the pupils' learning process.

The **Focus** books are also investigational in approach. They are more closely aligned to the National Curriculum Attainment Targets for Mathematics. Tasks are fairly short and are mostly designed to be completed during one or two class lessons. They are clearly described in terms of their mathematical nature, for example:

● 'Below zero' (from *Number — Extension*, levels 5 – 7, Unit 6)
● 'Symmetry' (from *Shape and Space — Core*, levels 3 – 5, Unit 7).

The reference to attainment levels in the Focus books is intended only as a guide — the levels should not dominate the allocation of books to pupils.

There is room for adventure! For example, if a pupil working on *Shape and Space — Lead-In* does the work on polygons particularly well, he or she would probably benefit from and enjoy tackling some of the work on polygons in *Shape and Space — Core* and possibly in the *Extension* book too. You might also use the *Lead-In* book on *Handling Data* to give experience in designing surveys, for example, which some pupils, irrespective of their ability, might not have had in their previous school.

Figure 1 shows the connections between Theme and Focus materials, with the role of computing clearly at the heart of *Century Maths*. Figure 2 illustrates how the Focus books serve the different year groups from Year 7 to Year 11. Figure 3 indicates the way in which the Focus books for Y7/8 encompass the National Curriculum through three level-spans: Lead-In, Core and Extension.

A key point in Figure 2 is that areas of overlap are provided in different books with appropriately different presentation and language according to the age of the pupil. For example, level 4 occurs first in the Core books for

Years 7 and 8, also for Year 9 and finally in the Lead-In book for Years 10 and 11. This is for students aged 11, 13 and 15 who might be working at the same level but with very different needs in terms of presentation and language.

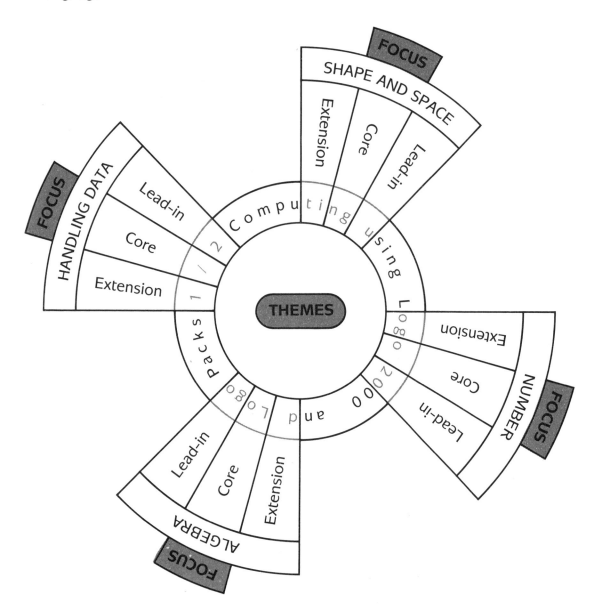

Figure 1 Linking Theme and Focus Books

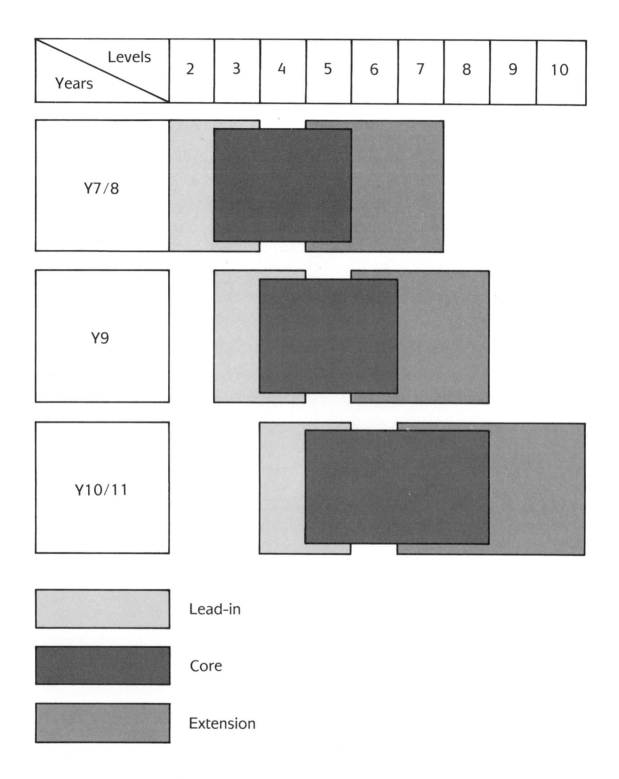

Figure 2 Focus Books for Years 7 to 11

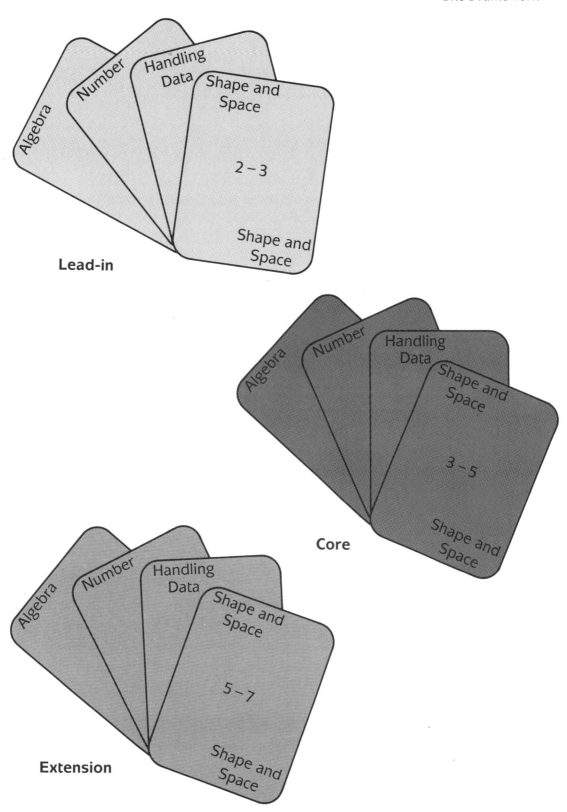

Figure 3 Focus Book Groupings for Years 7 and 8

Links between Theme and Focus

The links between Theme and Focus materials are repeated in the Teacher's Notes.

Teachers will vary in the way they choose to use the two types of material — some will start with a Theme, spend, say, three weeks on it and then strengthen or extend the mathematics involved by some further work from the indicated Focus book. Others may prefer to establish the mathematical foundations using the Focus books first, then move to the appropriate Theme (chosen according to the likely mathematics content as indicated in the Teacher's Notes) to apply the mathematics already learned. (See p.18, Teaching Styles and Approaches.)

A Note on the Detailed Focus References

The Focus references provide a useful platform for:

- **planning** the follow-up work if you start with a Theme
- **preparation** if you choose to start with the Focus material.

For example, in the Theme *Neighbourhood*, the section 'Town Trail' includes the following Focus reference:

Scale drawing and ratio

	LI	C	E
Number	8	7,13	4,9
Shape and space		7	6

This indicates the units in the Lead-In (LI), Core (C) and Extension (E) Focus books for *Number* and *Shape and Space*, where the appropriate follow-up material can be found.

Link Pages

Each pupil's Theme has a page indicating what mathematics may have been experienced within the Theme. Under each heading, unit references are given for more work on these particular topics in the appropriate Focus books, Lead-In, Core and Extension. The Teacher's Notes have these references for each section of the Theme. Examples of these references are given below.

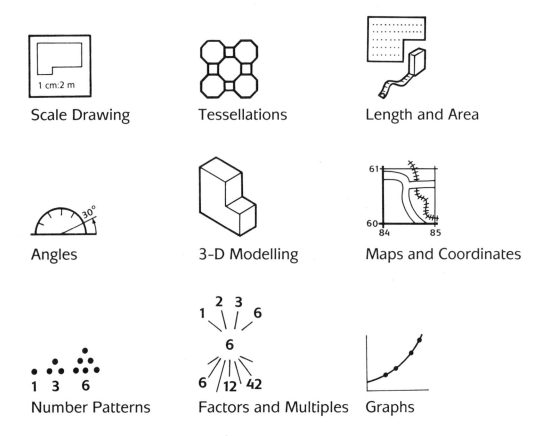

Scale Drawing

Tessellations

Length and Area

Angles

3-D Modelling

Maps and Coordinates

Number Patterns

Factors and Multiples

Graphs

The references could be to material which:

- would be helpful in carrying out the work in the Theme
- would develop skill in the mathematics learned
- sets the mathematics in another context, thereby enabling the pupil to identify and abstract the mathematics (e.g. after using Ratio in 'Recipes' in the *Food* Theme, it can be used in 'Scale Drawing' in the *Number* Focus material)
- gives further developments which would be of interest to the pupils.

Why Include Link Pages in the Pupils' Books?

- It enables pupils to identify, **for themselves**, the mathematics that they are using.
- It enables pupils to use their own initiative in learning — they may use the references to find help **as they develop the work** within the theme.

In general, giving pupils knowledge of the connecting material should encourage a feeling of self-confidence in the progress they are making.

Using Teacher's Support Packs

Teacher's notes are presented in booklets containing double-page spreads for each section of pupil material. This provides for easy reference on your desk. Each Theme and Focus book has an associated *Teacher's Support Pack* which contains:

- specific teacher's notes relating to the Theme books and Focus books
- guidance on problem-solving in the classroom
- further ideas for problem-solving activities
- direct links to the National Curriculum
- guidance on assessment and record-keeping
- cross-curricular links and guidance

Supplementary worksheets required by the pupils are published in the *Century Maths Worksheet Pack*. Teacher's notes for the **Themes** will show:

- main activities
- materials required
- computing references (Logo 2000 documentation and LogoPack)
- scope for mathematics development
- teaching suggestions
- links with focus texts
- cross-curricular links to other subject areas/cross-curricular themes

Possible links with National Curriculum Statements of Attainment are also indicated. The outcome of Theme work obviously depends on choices by you and/or your pupils and the directions in which different groups of pupils take their investigations. Therefore the links with the National Curriculum are those seen as direct links by the authors.

Materials required are listed, with icons to show whether they are essential or simply 'helpful if available'. A list of the icons used is given above (p.7).

Example (from Neighbourhood)

Materials required

 Worksheets 1 – 3:

'A walkabout tour of Newark on Trent' 1, 2

'Street plan for Newark Town Centre' 3

 Maps of area around the school
Tracing paper
Card

Teaching Suggestions

This is probably the main section in the teacher's material. It includes a general description of the kind of activity to expect — for example, the Theme may involve some time spent out-of-doors or there may be measuring, graph-drawing or carrying out a survey in the school. It is usually divided into:

- the general approach
- 'starting off'
- the main activities

There may be some comment on extension ideas suggested in the pupils' book. The 'starting off' section often gives ideas for the initial group discussion and ways of organising the groups.

Teacher's notes for the **Focus** books are similar to those for the Theme books. Each unit within a Focus book has a double-page spread of information relating to that unit.

Once again, the double-page spreads contain a variety of information:

- lists of materials required by the pupils
- teaching suggestions for developing the particular unit
- guidance on solutions and/or sets of answers
- links with the National Curriculum, indicating the Statements of Attainment covered within the unit.

Using Computing

Within *Century Maths*, there are two aspects to the use of the computer, both connected and dealing with the use of Logo. Materials have been written specifically for *Century Maths* and are referenced throughout the pupils' and teacher's books by the icon shown below:

Century Maths LogoPack 1 is a package of photocopiable activities designed for use by pupils of all abilities. The aim of the materials is to introduce pupils to the important aspects of the Logo language in the context of solving mathematical problems and using mathematical ideas.

The materials are not intended to be used in a linear sequence, but partial ordering within the materials is apparent.

The activities are grouped as follows:

(B) Beginning Logo commands
(P) Procedures
(O) Other useful commands
(S) Superprocedures
(V) Using variables to define general procedures
(T) Turtle turn and angle
(A) Arithmetic
(R) Ratio and proportion
(F) Functions
(C) Coordinates
(G) Graphs
(SY) Symmetry/Transformations
(RR) Spirals/Recursion

All activities are written for the **BBC Master** and **Acorn Archimedes** computers, with added commands for the **RM Nimbus** where these are at variance with those for the BBC Master.

Comprehensive teacher's notes are included in the package.

The second area of computer support for *Century Maths* is through the *Century Maths* Software Package **Logo 2000.**

Logo 2000 provides materials, including software, which make Logo the natural working computer environment for many of the mathematical problems which teachers and pupils might want to solve. This package develops the excitement of Logo by bringing the same feelings to database, spreadsheet and graph-plotting problems. This is achieved through three integrated pieces of software, available on one disk:

● **LogoBase** gives pupils the power of a database, allied to the control and flexibility associated with Logo. The pupils use the Logo language together with the extra commands provided to create and manipulate their own data.
● **LogoSheet** allows pupils to use Logo for spreadsheet activities, but maintains the exploratory nature of Logo itself.
● **LogoPlotter,** another extension of Logo, allows the pupil to graph functions and produce statistical charts. Data from LogoBase or LogoSheet might be graphed into LogoPlotter.

Pupils are able to move easily between the three components within a Logo environment.

Logo 2000 includes documentation aimed at pupils to enable them to get started, as well as full details of the software for the more advanced user. A number of ideas cards designed to stimulate projects are also included.

Throughout *Century Maths* pupils are encouraged to use *Logo 2000* either as a tool for solving or aiding the solution of a problem or to create their own projects and explore the files on the disk. This is endorsed within the texts by a series of icons used to refer pupils to particular parts of the *Logo 2000* disk and documentation.

Logo 2000 is available first for the Archimedes, with a version for the RM Nimbus due in 1992. (The RM Nimbus version will be compatible with that used within the *Century Maths LogoPack 1*.)

Apart from *LogoPack 1* and *Logo 2000*, references to other software packages are made in the pupils' materials and *Teacher's Support Packs*. These references supply information relating to software allied to a particular activity, which the authors feel will enhance the pupils' experience.

Flexibility

Teaching Styles and Approaches

There are probably as many different mathematics teaching approaches as there are teachers but, in general, most teachers seem to find a balance between:

- learning through the solving of problems
- the direct learning of specific mathematics topics.

The *Century Maths* philosophy offers the Themes, which give opportunities for solving problems which may be new to the learner, and backs this up with the Focus books which provide the mathematics content. How the emphasis is placed is really your decision, and you may wish to change the emphasis according to the different needs throughout the school year. For example, as examinations approach, concentration on mathematics topics might be appropriate, while problem-solving experience, involving as it does discussion, decision-making and planning of work, may seem more suitable when there is less pressure of time.

In trialling *Century Maths* we found considerable variation in teaching styles. Some teachers used the Themes as the main source of learning, following these with concentration on the mathematics concepts and skills which had arisen. Others said they would prefer to spend a shorter time on a section of a Theme and alternate this with some direct mathematics learning from the Focus books. At the other extreme, the mathematics topics would be learned first and then applied to the solving of problems.

In the following pages we give an example of the way you might start with the learning in a Theme and follow with specific related topics from the Focus book (Figure 4), or alternatively (Figure 5), you might use the Focus book first and then extend into the different sections of a Theme and apply the appropriate mathematics.

The Choice is Yours . . .

Example A: *'Start with the problem — then create the mathematics'*
Is this your approach? You offer (i) a situation requiring activity which must be planned and/or (ii) a problem requiring solution so that your class decide

what is needed and then, quite possibly, extend the mathematics they already know to meet the requirements.

If so, your way of using *Century Maths* could be to choose a Theme which provides broadly the range of mathematical experiences that you find appropriate for your class. It is likely that, in using the Theme, different groups in the class will learn slightly different mathematical skills and concepts, according to the directions they choose.

Your follow-up would be to select appropriate Focus books, to clarify and/or extend the mathematics learned. In selecting the Focus books you will find recommendations in the teacher's notes for each section of the Theme; references are also included in the pupils' texts.

For example: you select the Theme *Food* for a Year 7 class. In the course of this work the pupils in different groups gain experience of number (permutations of small numbers), number patterns, equivalent fractions, money, measurement of space, handling data (sorting, survey), formulae and spreadsheets as well as planning and decision-making (inherent in any Theme).

From Figure 4 it is clear that you can follow this up with the Focus books *Number, Shape and Space, Handling Data* and some *Algebra*, according to the mathematics experienced, and at the appropriate level. (Pages 38–42 provide black-line masters which may be photocopied on to acetates to show the build-up of part of this diagram.)

Example B: *'Learn the mathematics — then apply it'*
With this approach you prepare for 'open-ended' work by taking your pupils through the main mathematical concepts that they are likely to encounter and then give them the opportunity to apply their knowledge to whatever problems are raised.

If this is your approach, your use of *Century Maths* would be to select the mathematics topics that you want from the Focus books and follow with one of the Themes which is likely to involve those concepts.

In Figure 5, examples are given of the way mathematics started in a Focus book can be followed up by applying it in the *Food* Theme.

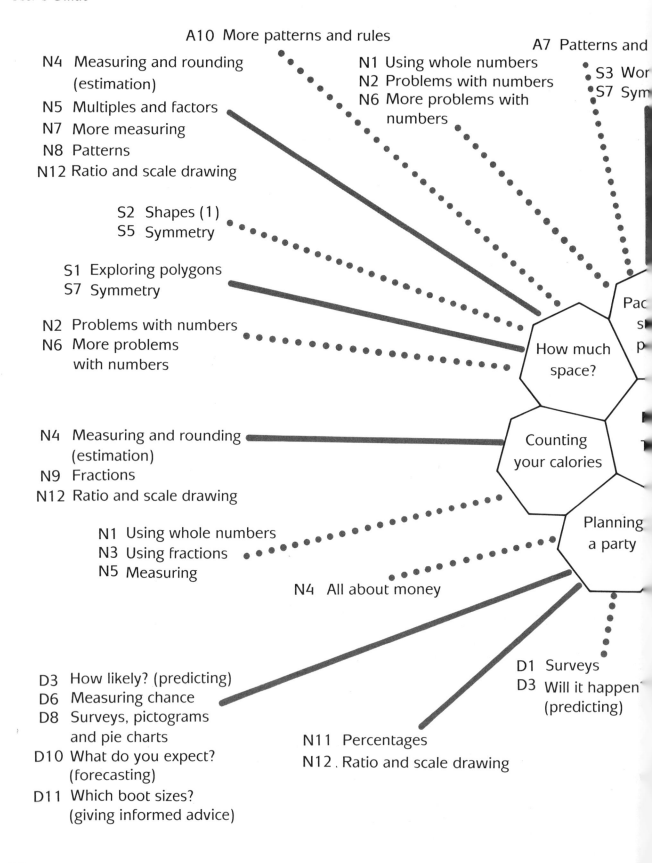

A10 More patterns and rules

N4 Measuring and rounding
(estimation)
N5 Multiples and factors
N7 More measuring
N8 Patterns
N12 Ratio and scale drawing

N1 Using whole numbers
N2 Problems with numbers
N6 More problems with
numbers

A7 Patterns and
S3 Wor
S7 Sym

S2 Shapes (1)
S5 Symmetry

S1 Exploring polygons
S7 Symmetry

N2 Problems with numbers
N6 More problems
with numbers

How much
space?

Pac
s
p

N4 Measuring and rounding
(estimation)
N9 Fractions
N12 Ratio and scale drawing

Counting
your calories

N1 Using whole numbers
N3 Using fractions
N5 Measuring

Planning
a party

N4 All about money

D3 How likely? (predicting)
D6 Measuring chance
D8 Surveys, pictograms
and pie charts
D10 What do you expect?
(forecasting)
D11 Which boot sizes?
(giving informed advice)

N11 Percentages
N12 . Ratio and scale drawing

D1 Surveys
D3 Will it happen
(predicting)

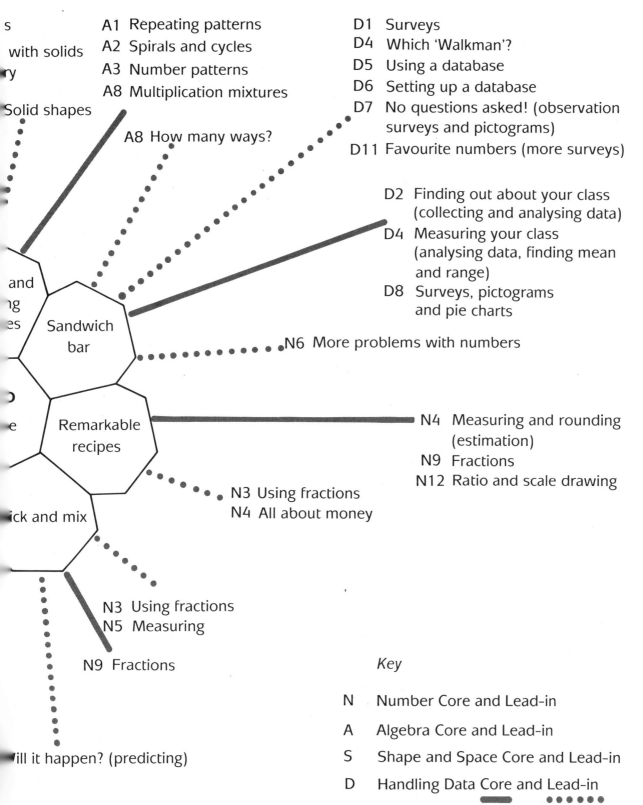

A1 Repeating patterns
A2 Spirals and cycles
A3 Number patterns
A8 Multiplication mixtures

A8 How many ways?

D1 Surveys
D4 Which 'Walkman'?
D5 Using a database
D6 Setting up a database
D7 No questions asked! (observation surveys and pictograms)
D11 Favourite numbers (more surveys)

s
with solids
ry
Solid shapes

and
ng
es

Sandwich bar

D2 Finding out about your class (collecting and analysing data)
D4 Measuring your class (analysing data, finding mean and range)
D8 Surveys, pictograms and pie charts

N6 More problems with numbers

)
e

Remarkable recipes

N4 Measuring and rounding (estimation)
N9 Fractions
N12 Ratio and scale drawing

ick and mix

N3 Using fractions
N4 All about money

N3 Using fractions
N5 Measuring

N9 Fractions

ill it happen? (predicting)

Key

N   Number Core and Lead-in

A   Algebra Core and Lead-in

S   Shape and Space Core and Lead-in

D   Handling Data Core and Lead-in

Figure 4 An Example of Theme-Focus Links

Figure 5 Focus-Theme Links (using the example of the theme book Food)

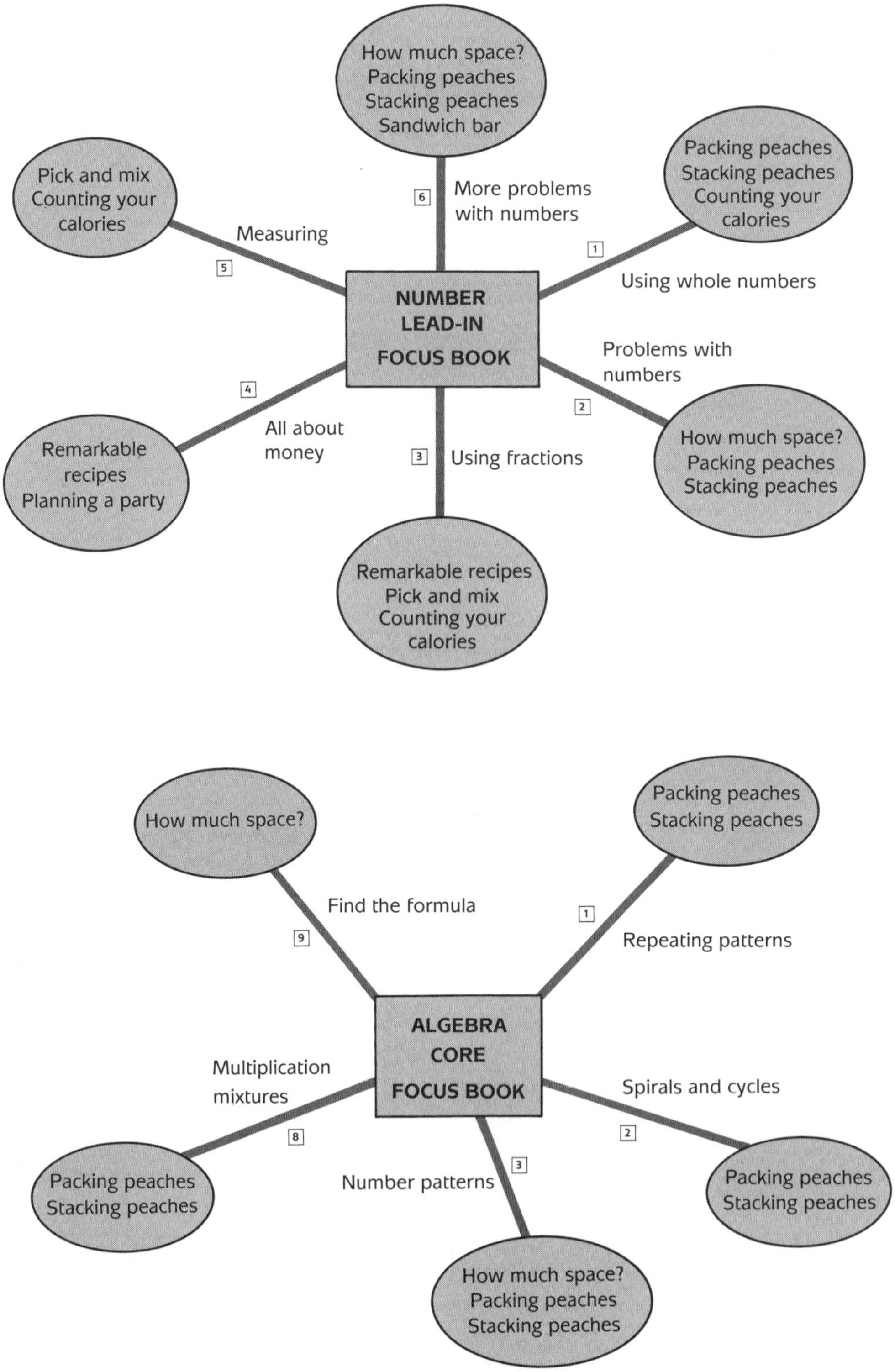

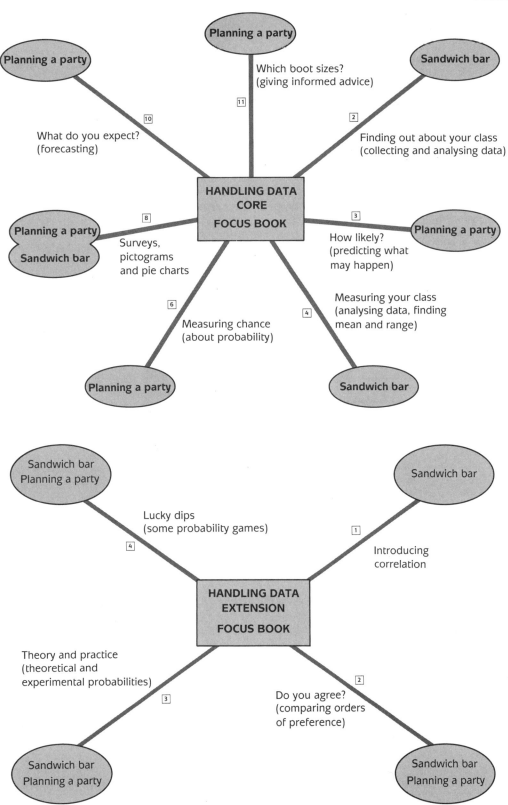

Assessment and record-keeping

In deciding on a procedure for assessment and record-keeping for *Century Maths* the following principles were observed:

The procedure should

- promote good practice in assessment and teaching
- be linked to the National Curriculum requirements
- involve pupils in monitoring their own progress
- be directly relevant to *Century Maths* materials
- be sufficiently flexible to accommodate possible LEA assessment schemes
- be helpful to busy teachers . . . and easy to use!

The result of these ideas is individual record sheets showing the **work in which the pupil has been involved** up to each Key Stage. This will be completed by the pupil but it is intended that the pupil should find the task meaningful and informative (not a 'ticking boxes' activity). The record sheet indicates the relationship to the Attainment Targets. At intervals you will have the opportunity to give an assessment of the success of that work.

How the Focus Books can help with Assessment

In order to relate pupils' work to the National Curriculum, the Focus books give clear indications of the relevant Attainment Target within ATs 2–8 and 10–14. While the pupils should feel confident that they can work freely and make mistakes (often useful, in terms of learning), you will be assimilating information about their progress from day to day. This information could be supplemented by testing where you feel this is necessary.

Themes and Assessment

The Themes provide clear opportunities for the demonstration of achievement in terms of Attainment Targets 1 and 9. These are normally considered rather difficult to assess, but assessment need not always be in written form and there is ample opportunity to observe and note the progress of pupils as they **plan mathematical work, explain their work and discuss strategies.** You cannot be with all the pupils at the same time but assessment by observation can certainly help to reduce the stress and unprofitable use of time that written examinations impose on pupils.

To help in identifying the areas occurring in the Themes which are listed in ATs 1 and 9, an assessment grid is included within each *Teacher's Support*

Pack for Theme material. The grid presents an analysis of the **planning, action** and **explanation** that you may observe while following a Theme in a classroom. This is presented at the different Attainment Levels. An 'extension' column allows you to consider pupils' work which has been taken to a deeper level of understanding. This grid forms part of the 'Record-keeping and Assessment' section, which supplies ideas and guidelines for assessing pupils' work, then provides for a suitable record of your findings, while at the same time retaining the spirit of 'open-endedness' and pupil involvement promoted throughout all the *Century Maths* materials.

Further Attainment Target references in the Themes are given in the *Teacher's Support Packs*, but because the Themes tend to be of an open-ended nature, it is assumed that different pupils will take the work in different directions. Work on Themes may continue over two or three weeks, so you will have time to note the experiences of individual pupils and to guide them to appropriate Focus books for extension work or to supply any necessary activity that has been missed.

Pathways through Century Maths *Themes*

Phase 1 — Years 7 and 8

On the following pages examples are given of ways of planning the use of the Themes in Years 7 and 8. Provided that the mathematics content is appropriate, the sequence is influenced by the suitability of the contexts to the children's experience, and this probably varies according to geographical and local conditions. With these ideas in mind you can make your own decision as to the best sequence for your class and, in doing this, the indications of direct mathematical experience attributed to the different Themes in the following pages should be helpful.

In making a selection we have based the choice of *Ourselves* for the start of Year 7, when pupils are new to the school, on the context which involves measuring each other and the furniture. We feel that this is a good way of getting children to work together fairly quickly and to get into the habit of discussing their methods. Another Theme which would be equally suitable at this stage would be *Animals*. We have placed it second in our sequence. Several religious and cultural feasts occur in the winter, which influenced our idea that *Festivals* could be placed either at the end of the autumn term or at the beginning of the spring term; we chose the latter. Some Themes could be allocated at any time according to local interest, e.g. *Patterns*, which we placed at the beginning of the summer term. It would probably be appropriate for most schools to have *School Fair* at the end of the summer term.

A similar analysis influenced the sequence shown for Year 8. For example, the *Trees* Theme involves some outdoor work and so it would be helpful to do this during the better weather.

Some aspects of mathematics content might suggest some changes in the sequence given. For example, there is a major algebra component in *Connections*. If your scheme of work requires algebra earlier in Year 8, you might decide to exchange this Theme for, say, *Traffic*.

Some direct mathematics links between Theme and Focus Books – Year 7

		AT1	Number	Algebra	AT9	Shape & Space	Handling Data
TERM 1	Ourselves	✓	measure, ratio		✓	scale drawing	surveys, collect, record and process data, interpretation, averages
	Animals	✓	proportion, measure (speed), logic	logic	✓	enlargement	representation
TERM 2	Festivals	✓	proportion, pattern	formulae	✓	pattern, transformation, polygons	
	Food	✓	operations, permutations, pattern	pattern, logic	✓	some links with number pattern	interpretation
TERM 3	Patterns		length, area		✓	angle, polygons, pattern, parallel lines, congruence, transformations, tessellations	
	School Fair	✓	proportion, money		✓	symmetry	random numbers, frequency, probability, representation, surveys

Some direct mathematics links between Theme and Focus Books – Year 8

		AT1	Number	Algebra	AT9	Shape & Space	Handling Data
TERM 1	*Trees*	✓	proportion, scale, measure	graphs	✓	angle, directions	
	Music	✓	fractions, measure (area), money	permutations	✓	directions	representation, interpretation, survey
TERM 2	*Traffic*	✓	distance, time, conversion	functions and graphs	✓	maps	collect, record and process data
	Neighbourhood	✓	measure, scale, proportion	coordinates	✓	scale drawing, plans, nets, maps, direction, symmetry, tessellations	
TERM 3	*Connections*	✓	operations, pattern	generalisation, coordinates, interpreting graphs, logic	✓	pattern	data representation
	Holidays	✓	measure, proportion, scale, conversion		✓	plans, nets, solids	using a table, representation

Setting up with Century Maths

There are two main ways in which *Century Maths* could be adopted by a mathematics department. These are either to consider both the Theme and Focus material or to look towards using one or other of these, in conjunction with existing material.

The calculations below provide a guide to **minimum** purchasing quantities for each of the two scenarios given above. All calculations are based on a mixed-ability year group of 120 pupils. In years 7, 8 and 9, it is assumed that they are taught in four mixed-ability groupings; in years 10 and 11, estimations have been made on the assumption that some form of setting is employed. The model selected for this purpose considers five sets of pupils being taught simultaneously.

The following assumptions have also been made:

- each of the year groups is taught as a whole year group, simultaneously
- no two year groups are taught at the same time
- there is no duplicate use of materials taken into account

Full implementation of Century Maths

Years 7 and 8: Mixed-ability groupings

Theme Books
Food/Animals   *Trees/Neighbourhood*
Festivals/School Fair   *Patterns/Ourselves*
Holidays/Traffic   *Music/Connections*

Quantities required:

For the first calculation, it is assumed that a whole class group concentrates on the same Theme:

18 copies of each of the six Theme books
Total number of copies: 108

This estimate is based on a variety of Themes being researched simultaneously within a single classroom:

8 copies of each Theme book
Total number of copies: 48

Focus Books
Quantities required:

	Number	*Shape & Space*	*Algebra*	*Handling Data*
Lead-In	4	4	4	4
Core	6	6	6	6
Extension	4	4	4	4

For either whole class or multi-Theme involvement in the Theme material, class groups will require the quantities given above.

Total number of copies per class: 56
Total number of copies per year group: 224

Teacher's Support Packs
Each pack comprises a set of referenced notes for each unit in each of the Theme and Focus books. The *Worksheet Pack* contains all the worksheets required for Years 7 and 8.

Quantities required:

1 copy of each *Teacher's Support Pack* per teacher
Total number of copies of *Teacher's Support Packs*: 56
(assuming 4 teachers in the department)

1 set of worksheet masters per department
Total number of sets of photocopy masters: 1

Logo 2000 and LogoPack 1

Quantities required:
1 of each per classroom

Year 9: Mixed-ability groupings

Themes*
Linkages/Measuring Devices   Growth   Cultural Mathematics
* At present, these are working titles and may therefore alter in due course.

Quantities required:

Considering the two scenarios as in Years 7 and 8, firstly for whole class involvement in a single Theme:

18 copies of each Theme Book
Total number of copies: 54

For the multi-Theme classroom, quantities would become:

8 copies of each Theme Book
Total number of copies: 24

Focus Books
Quantities required:

	Number	Shape & Space	Algebra	Handling Data
Lead-In	4	4	4	4
Core	6	6	6	6
Extension	4	4	4	4

Total number of copies per year group: 224

Teacher's Support Packs
As for Years 7 and 8, these materials will be supplied as *Teacher's Support Packs* with an allied *Worksheet Pack*.

1 copy of each *Teacher's Support Pack*
Total number of copies of *Teacher's Support Packs*: 60
1 set of worksheet masters per department

Years 10 and 11 (Assuming some form of setting involved)

All of the quantities given in this section refer to the total number of units required to equip one year group.

Theme Books

For years 10 and 11 there will be: one *Theme Starter Manual* and two *Theme Books* which will be written particularly to address cross-curricular work. On the assumption that minimum quantities are used, 1 copy of a Theme Book per two pupils should suffice.

Total number of copies: 60

Focus Books
Quantities required:

	Number	Shape & Space	Algebra	Handling Data
Lead-In	20	20	20	20
Core	50	50	50	50
Extension	20	20	20	20

Total number of copies per year group: 360

Teacher's Support Packs
Criteria will be as for Year 9.
Quantities required:
> 1 copy of each *Teacher's Support Pack* per teacher
> **Total number of Teacher's Support Packs: 60**
> **1 set of worksheet masters per department**

Part Implementation of *Century Maths*

Having considered the full implementation in detail, it is relatively easy to extract, from the details given, the quantities required if a school intends introducing either the Theme or Focus material individually. However, when selecting one or other of the strands of *Century Maths* in isolation, it is advisable to purchase the *Teacher's Support Packs* and the Logo materials.

Century Maths *and* Departmental *INSET*

Within mathematics departments, teachers are seeking ways to enhance and develop the teaching and learning of mathematics, while at the same time keeping the National Curriculum firmly in mind. *Century Maths* provides a vehicle which can be used to accommodate the most discerning teacher — or pupil — by its very structure. The essence of *Century Maths* is the ethos of 'working together' and such an ethos need not apply to the pupils alone. Through co-operation and discussion, a department can work in concert to develop ideas germinated within *Century Maths*. This allows *Century Maths* to be seen as a resource that can become the catalyst for developing mathematical ideas beyond the scope of the books themselves.

Food for thought . . .

As a department, try to establish the role of INSET within the framework of the department. At all times, try to maintain a perspective of what role *Century Maths* has, within the answer to each of these questions:

- How often do you meet as a department?
- How long are these meetings?
- Are they structured?
- Who decides what to talk about?
- Are curriculum matters subsumed by administrative chores?

If, as a department, you meet on a regular basis, the agenda for the meetings might include such items as:

- mathematical ideas — developing some aspects of mathematics that may lead to curriculum change
- the teaching and learning of mathematics — expressing ideas relating to aspects of your teaching environment that produced a particular learning or teaching strategy
- cross-curricular links with other subject areas
- general departmental administration

Making the first move . . .

From the outset, it is important to reflect on the fact that lasting progress from school-based INSET will involve three main elements. These are:

- personal change
- inter-personal change
- curriculum change

Personal change could involve answering questions such as

'Have you considered another viewpoint to your own about . . . ?'
'Am I, or are we, happy with the way we are teaching at the moment?'
'Shall I try this new idea, even though I am not convinced?'

This is extremely difficult to do, but if lasting, meaningful curriculum change is to be seen, then these questions need answering.

Inter-personal change could involve considering these questions:

'Do I talk about mathematics teaching with others in the department?'
'Do I know how others in the department overcome this problem?'
'Do I talk to colleagues in other departments to plan joint work?'

Through communicating with each other and trying to understand different viewpoints, there is every chance of success without any feelings of resentment arising.

The aspect of curriculum change is concerned with the process of identifying and resolving problems related to the mathematical curriculum being delivered in your school.

Where does *Century Maths* fit in?

Through the structure of the material, *Century Maths* has considerable flexibility. One measure of this flexibility is the facility to use the material as a stimulus for discussions dealing with curriculum change within departmental meetings.

Activity

Look at the following diagram. All arrows have been omitted. The heart of the diagram is the concept of **Learning**. Other aspects are those associated with the task of learning mathematics.

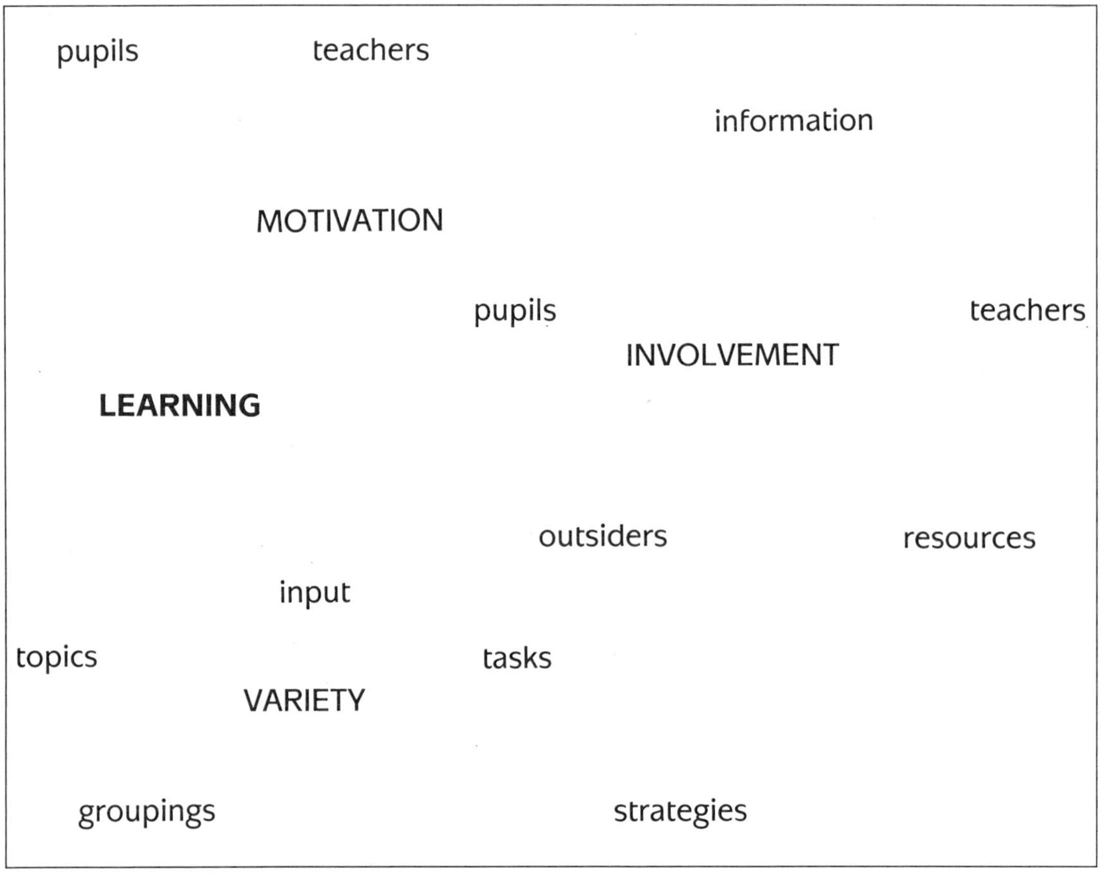

```
pupils          teachers

                                    information

        MOTIVATION

                pupils                          teachers
                    INVOLVEMENT
    LEARNING


                    outsiders           resources
        input
topics                  tasks
        VARIETY

    groupings                   strategies
```

- Place arrows in the diagram to display all the possible links. (You may photocopy the diagram if you wish to.)
- Discuss the links you have made with the rest of the department.
- Is there any composite diagram that the whole department can accept?

Activity

Consider the strategies strand of the diagram.

- List all the strategies that you regard as essential in the learning of mathematics.
- Compare your list with those compiled by the rest of the department.
- Can you create an agreed list of strategies?
- Are you happy that your existing mode of delivery of the mathematics curriculum develops all of these agreed strategies effectively?

Within the strategies strand, had you considered the following?

reporting	co-operating	talking	planning
testing	researching	checking	doing

All of these strategies are extensively developed within *Century Maths* and are seen to be of paramount importance. For example:

Activity

Consider the activity on p.31 of the Theme *Neighbourhood*.

Now, having read the activity, try to decide which of the listed strategies can be observed within this activity.

- Itemise where they occur.
- How can you develop this activity beyond the ideas given in the teaching suggestions?

Activity

Look at the following statements:

AT 9, Level 5
- select the materials and the mathematics to use for a task; check there is sufficient information; work methodically and review progress
- interpret mathematical information presented in oral, written or visual form
- make and test simple statements

AT 11, Level 5
- use networks to solve problems
- specify location by means of coordinates in the four quadrants

AT 12, Level 6
- design and use a questionnaire to survey opinion (taking account of bias); collate and analyse results

Consider the extracts given above and design a piece of work to supplement the 'Town Trail' activity. Try to take account of some or all of the processes listed above.

- Can this process be repeated within other areas of the *Neighbourhood* Theme?
- Can further areas of the National Curriculum be clearly observed within this Theme, other than those illustrated within the teacher's notes?
- What possibilities exist for good cooperation with teachers from other departments?

Clearly, the process above is an exemplar of what is possible within *Century Maths*. This is one of many avenues that can be explored in INSET time. The structure of the department, the teaching personnel and the learning environment are only three of the facets to be considered when using *Century Maths* as a vehicle for curriculum development. All these aspects are unique to each individual school and must be treated accordingly.

Footnote

In appreciation of the uniqueness of each department and its needs, and the belief in supporting departments to use *Century Maths* effectively, INSET support is available through the channels mentioned on p.4 of this *User's Guide*. Help us to help you by keeping in touch and feeding back your thoughts — and concerns — about using *Century Maths*.

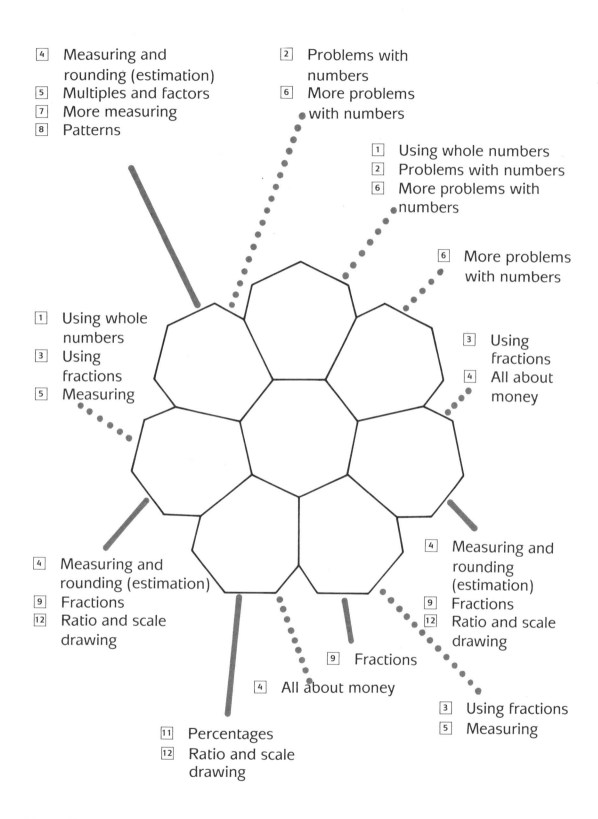

4 Measuring and rounding (estimation)
5 Multiples and factors
7 More measuring
8 Patterns

2 Problems with numbers
6 More problems with numbers

1 Using whole numbers
2 Problems with numbers
6 More problems with numbers

6 More problems with numbers

1 Using whole numbers
3 Using fractions
5 Measuring

3 Using fractions
4 All about money

4 Measuring and rounding (estimation)
9 Fractions
12 Ratio and scale drawing

4 Measuring and rounding (estimation)
9 Fractions
12 Ratio and scale drawing

9 Fractions

4 All about money

3 Using fractions
5 Measuring

11 Percentages
12 Ratio and scale drawing

Food *Theme linked to* Number – *Lead-in and Core*

1 Repeating patterns
2 Spirals and cycles
3 Number patterns
8 Multiplication mixtures

7 Patterns and rules

8 How many ways?

10 More patterns and rules

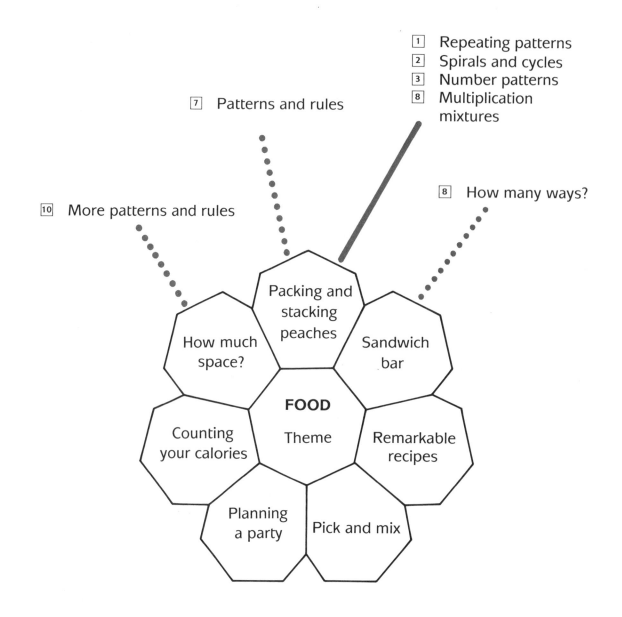

Food *Theme linked to* Algebra *– Lead-in and Core*

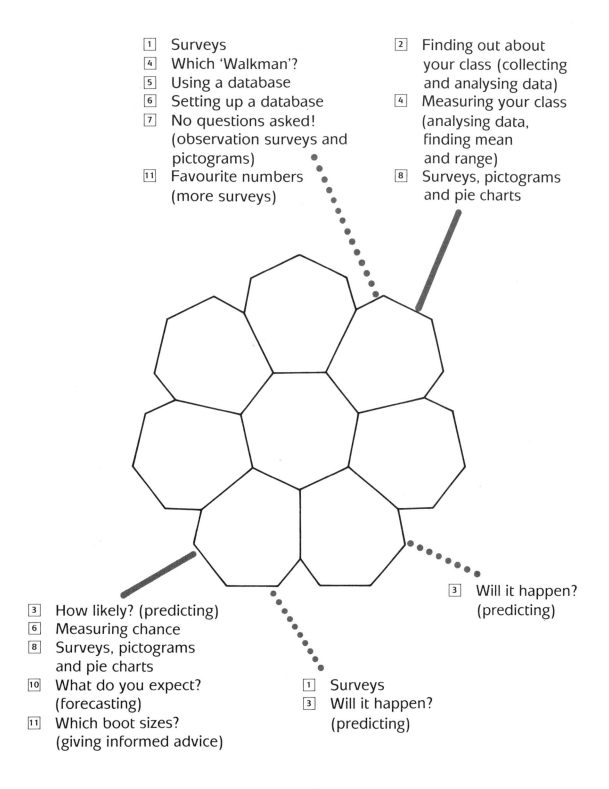

1. Surveys
4. Which 'Walkman'?
5. Using a database
6. Setting up a database
7. No questions asked! (observation surveys and pictograms)
11. Favourite numbers (more surveys)

2. Finding out about your class (collecting and analysing data)
4. Measuring your class (analysing data, finding mean and range)
8. Surveys, pictograms and pie charts

3. How likely? (predicting)
6. Measuring chance
8. Surveys, pictograms and pie charts
10. What do you expect? (forecasting)
11. Which boot sizes? (giving informed advice)

1. Surveys
3. Will it happen? (predicting)

3. Will it happen? (predicting)

Food *Theme linked to* Handling Data – *Lead-in and Core*

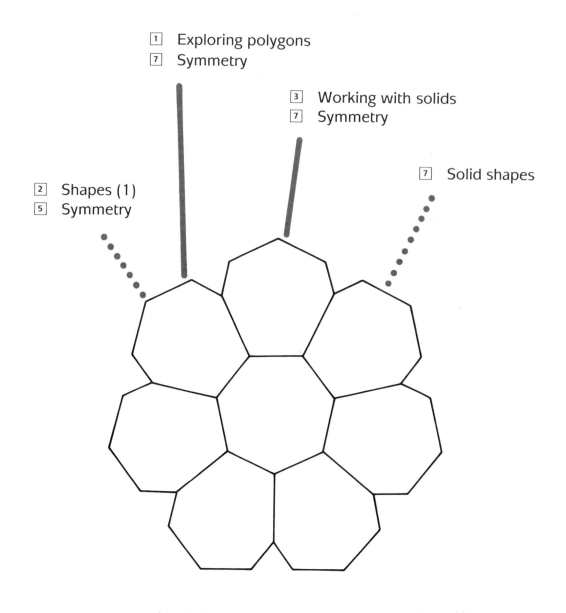

1. Exploring polygons
7. Symmetry

3. Working with solids
7. Symmetry

7. Solid shapes

2. Shapes (1)
5. Symmetry

Food *Theme linked to* Shape and Space *— Lead-in and Core*

Century Maths publishing programme

	Y7/8	Y9	Y10/11

THEME	Food/
	   Animals
	Trees/
	   Neighbourhood
	Festivals/
	   School Fair
	Patterns/
	   Ourselves
	Holidays/
	   Traffic
	Music/
	   Connections
	
	Two Theme Teacher's
	Support Packs
		Growth
		
		Cultural Maths
		
		Measuring Devices/
		Linkages
		
		Theme Teacher's
		Support Pack
			Four cross-curricular
			Themes
			
			Theme 'starter' book
			
			Theme Teacher's
			Support Pack

FOCUS	*Core* *Lead-in* *Extension* 3 – 5 2 – 3 5 – 7 NUMBER 3 – 5 2 – 3 5 – 7 ALGEBRA 3 – 5 2 – 3 5 – 7 SHAPE AND SPACE 3 – 5 2 – 3 5 – 7 HANDLING DATA	*Core* *Lead-in* *Extension* 4 – 6 3 – 4 6 – 8 NUMBER 4 – 6 3 – 4 6 – 8 ALGEBRA 4 – 6 3 – 4 6 – 8 SHAPE AND SPACE 4 – 6 3 – 4 6 – 8 HANDLING DATA	*Core* *Lead-in* *Extension* 5 – 8 4 – 5 7 – 10 NUMBER 5 – 8 4 – 5 7 – 10 ALGEBRA 5 – 8 4 – 5 7 – 10 SHAPE AND SPACE 5 – 8 4 – 5 7 – 10 HANDLING DATA
	Teacher's Support Pack for *each* Focus Book		
	Worksheet Pack	Worksheet Pack	Worksheet Pack

LOGO	Logo 2000
	   Archimedes
	
	LogoPack 1
		Logo 2000
		   Nimbus
			LogoPack 2